HOUSE TRAINING

R
RINGPRESS

Ringpress Books
©INTERPET Publishing
Vincent Lane, Dorking, Surrey,
RH4 3YX, England.

ISBN 1 86054 286 7

First published 2001. All rights reserved.

CARTOONS: Russell Jones.

DESIGN: Rob Benson & Sara Howell.

Printed and bound in Hong Kong through Printworks International Limited

INTRODUCTION ───────────── **4**
Basic instinct; Right age; Regular routine.

GETTING STARTED ───────────── **6**
Bingo!; Rewarding experience; Fun and games.

CLEANING UP ───────────── **8**
Good habits; Health check.

SPOTTING THE SIGNS ───────────── **10**

IN-HOUSE TRAINING ───────────── **12**
Size matters; Crate routine; Paper-training.

MAKING PROGRESS ───────────── **16**
Out and about; Time out; Two steps forward;
One step back.

WHEN ACCIDENTS HAPPEN ───────────── **20**
Out with the old; Not guilty; Positive behaviour;
Submissive urination.

SCENT-MARKING ───────────── **24**
Tackling the cause.

RESCUED DOGS ───────────── **26**
Never trained; Anxious wetters; Hope.

PROBLEM SOLVING ───────────── **28**
Fair weather friend; Baby blues.

OVER TO YOU ───────────── **32**

CONTENTS

INTRODUCTION

House-training is the part of puppyhood that many owners dread most, but there is no getting away from it! Nobody likes finding puddles and other accidents around the house, so the sooner you get started with your training, the better.

BASIC INSTINCT

Puppies have an age-old instinct to be clean in their 'den'. This relates to their ancestry in the wild, when pups were at risk from predators. They were easy prey, and evidence of their whereabouts, such as urine or faeces, would lead predators straight to the den. For this reason, the mother would regularly move the litter, and the pups learnt to soil away from where they ate and slept. This survival instinct can be used to your advantage when training the pup not to soil his *new* den – your house! (See Crate-training, page 12.)

RIGHT AGE

There is a popular myth that very young pups are too small to be trained. But just because they are small, it doesn't mean their brains don't work! In fact, young pups are far more receptive

to training than older ones, who are likely to have already developed some bad habits.

Your puppy's breeder may have started to teach the litter to be house-trained. It is important to continue this training the moment you bring your new pup home and to get into your own routine straightaway.

REGULAR ROUTINE

Routine is the key to successful house-training. Although pups can be unpredictable creatures and get themselves into all sorts of unexpected mischief, they are refreshingly reliable where their toilet habits are concerned. All pups, whatever their breed, sex or age, will be prone to relieving themselves at the following times:

• As soon as they wake up
• After eating
• After or during exercise/play
• When meeting new people
• When excited or nervous.

When it comes to these times, take your puppy outside to relieve himself. Pre-empting his actions will mean he is never given an opportunity to make a mistake.

GETTING STARTED

Choose a spot in your garden where you would like your pup to eliminate. It could be a grassy area behind a garden screen, or a corner of a paved patio. Take your puppy to this chosen spot regularly, and wait patiently for him to perform. It may take a while for him to do so, but don't hurry back indoors, give him time. If, after ten minutes or so, he still fails to relieve himself, take him indoors. Keep a close eye on him in case he is caught short, and try again in another half an hour.

BINGO!

When your pup does eventually relieve himself outside, say a command, such as "Get busy", or something similar. Use this command every time he eliminates, and your pup will soon learn what it means. You can then go on to train him to relieve himself as soon as you say the command.

REWARDING EXPERIENCE

When your pup has finished his business, praise him handsomely, and reward him for his good behaviour. Give him a small treat to show your appreciation, and play a game in the garden together before returning indoors. Positive, reward-based training not only helps your pup to learn what is required of him, it also benefits your relationship. It shows your pup that you are a kind, fair person, who gives praise where it is due, and that you are fun and exciting to be with.

FUN AND GAMES

It is important not to rush indoors as soon as the pup has done his business. If you do, the pup will soon learn to keep his legs crossed in order to gain more fun time outside in the garden! Your puppy should associate going to the toilet with a fun, enjoyable experience, not as a punishment (i.e. the end of his fun-time outside), so always reward and praise him once he has performed.

CLEANING UP

Once the praise and rewards have been given, clean up after your dog straightaway. It's not the most pleasant job in the world, but you will soon get used to it. Use a thick plastic bag (pet stores often sell handy-sized ones) – but make sure it does not have any air holes in it!

- Put your hand in the bag.
- Grab the offending material.
- Then pull your hand out of the bag, so that the faeces ends up inside it.
- Knot the top of the bag.
- Deposit it in a suitable bin (parks usually provide special dog bins).
- Wash your hands.

Reward your puppy with a game after he has performed correctly.

GOOD HABITS

Get yourself into the habit of clearing up after your pup while he is still eliminating in your garden. Even if it is raining outside, it is as well to get into good habits and to clear up immediately. Not only is it more hygienic, it saves more work in the long term, and will also benefit your dog's training. Dogs are essentially clean animals (honestly!) and he will be loathe to eliminate on his house-training spot if it is dirty and soiled.

Never leave home without bags in your pocket. Pick up after your dog without fail. Leaving your dog's mess in a public place is not only unpleasant and inconsiderate to others, it harms the reputation of all other dogs and dog owners, and provides ammunition to the anti-dog lobby. Some sweet souls feel so strongly about scooping poop, they even pick up other dogs' mess. This wouldn't be necessary if everyone took responsibility for their own dogs.

Responsible ownership means cleaning up after your dog.

HEALTH CHECK

Having such regular contact with your dog's faeces does have its advantages – honestly! It will enable you to monitor any changes in colour and solidity that can often signal ill-health or food intolerance. If you have any concerns, seek immediate veterinary advice.

9

SPOTTING THE SIGNS

As well as taking your puppy outside at designated times throughout the day (see page 5), you should remain vigilant just in case the pup is caught short. A puppy that is desperate to relieve himself may start sniffing the ground, and circling round and round before squatting.

A puppy that has previously been told off for having an accident is likely to be more covert and will seek out corners, or quiet, private places to relieve himself. Your former displeasure will have taught him that you do not approve of him answering a call of nature. As a result, he will do his best to avoid you catching him in the act. This is why it is so important never to punish the pup for what is only natural behaviour.

As soon as you see your puppy sniffing the ground or squatting, remain calm and simply whisk him

Be vigilant for the warning signs – such as sniffing the ground and circling.

outside. Call him to the back door using a friendly, jolly tone of voice, and encourage him into the garden. Then take him to his toileting area, and give the command word. As ever, you should give lots of lavish praise when he performs.

If you catch the puppy mid-flow, then startle him into stopping. Do not shout, as you do not want to appear angry; rather, you want to surprise your pup so he stops long enough for you to encourage him outside. A high-pitched squeak, a hand-clap, or a pretend sneeze will often do the trick. Once outside, follow the usual house-training routine of command, praise, and play.

TRAINING TIP

Remember, if your puppy has an accident, it is because he hasn't been given sufficient opportunity to relieve himself. Review your house-training schedule and slot in a few more trips outside in the future, so that the puppy is never forced to have an accident again.

IN-HOUSE TRAINING

Make sure you get a crate that will be big enough to accommodate an adult dog.

Crates are invaluable pieces of equipment. Not only do they provide a safe place where you can put your pup for short periods when he cannot be supervised (e.g. at night), but they can also aid his house-training development. They should never be used for long periods, nor should they become 'sin bins' where the pup is put if he has been naughty. Rather, the pup's crate should be his own cosy little den – a place to call his own, where he can rest undisturbed or gnaw his favourite chew in peace.

SIZE MATTERS
You must make sure that the crate is large enough for your pup. It is wise to purchase one that will comfortably accommodate your dog when he is fully grown, or you will have to keep replacing it as your puppy grows. The crate supplier will be able to advise you on the best sizes.

The crate should be large enough to contain a sleeping area for your pup, a heavy water bowl (that can't be tipped over easily), and a toileting area in case your puppy can't hold on throughout the night. This toileting area should be at the farthest point away from the puppy's bedding, as it will distress the pup considerably if he feels he is soiling his sleeping quarters. The toileting area should consist of lots of absorbent newspaper, that can be easily removed and replaced.

CRATE ROUTINE

Supplying a toileting area in the crate doesn't mean you can become a little lazy – your rigid toileting regime should still be followed to the letter. Just because your pup can use an area in his crate, doesn't mean you should encourage him to go there unless he really has to (the first few weeks after you bring your puppy home, for example, his bladder may not be strong enough to hold on through the night), as, every time he dirties his crate, his house-training progress takes a step backwards.

Even though you are using a crate, you must still stick to the regime of taking your puppy out at regular intervals.

You must still take your puppy outside last thing at night, and first thing in the early morning, so reducing the chances of him needing to relieve himself when he is confined – remember, the ideal place for your pup to eliminate is in the garden.

Some owners set their alarm to get up in the middle of the night to take the pup outside. However, it can be disruptive to the puppy's night-time routine and may encourage the pup to howl throughout the night for your attention! All puppies are individual – see what works best for your pup.

PAPER-TRAINING

Many owners have house-trained their puppies by using this method. The principle behind it is to choose a room where the puppy will initially spend most of his time – such as the kitchen – and to cover the floor with newspaper. The puppy will have no choice but to eliminate on newspaper. Gradually, as the puppy gets older, the area of newspaper is reduced, until, eventually, there is only a small area by the back door that the puppy uses as his toilet area. Then, the newspaper is taken to just outside the back door. The size of the paper is again reduced until it is no longer used, and the puppy is reliably eliminating outside in the garden.

Although this method has been shown to work, it is a somewhat laborious process – why train your puppy to eliminate on paper indoors when your ultimate aim is to teach him to eliminate outside? Why not teach him to go outside from the very start?

Paper-training is a progressive method of teaching your puppy to be clean in the house.

MAKING PROGRESS

OUT AND ABOUT

Once your puppy will reliably relieve himself on his toileting spot, you should add some variety. Once he knows his command words (e.g. "Be clean"), you should be able to instruct your puppy to 'go' anywhere. This may seem a petty thing to rehearse, but there is nothing more infuriating than going for a long country walk, with a dog who is fit to burst but refuses to urinate on anything other than paving slabs!

Once your puppy is eliminating on command, introduce him to the following surfaces:

- Concrete
- Tarmac
- Sand
- Gravel
- Grass
- Shingle

OH NO! NOT THE GRAVEL!!

Gradually reduce the number of times you take your puppy out.

As with the pup's initial toilet-training, give him the command word, and, when he relieves himself, give lots of praise and a treat, followed by a game or a walk. Remember, do not take your puppy anywhere where other dogs have been until he is fully inoculated.

TIME OUT

As your puppy gets older, so his capacity to control his bladder and bowels will increase. You will gradually be able to cut down on the number of times you routinely take the puppy outside, perhaps taking him out every three hours instead of every two. Then, slowly progress to taking him out every four hours, instead of three. But this should not be rushed, or you could end up with accidents in the house. If your pup is ever caught short, increase the number of times you take him outside until you reach the right balance again.

TWO STEPS FORWARD

After a couple of weeks, your puppy may let you know when he wants to go outside to eliminate. When he does this (by whimpering or barking at the back door, or getting your attention and leading you – Lassie-like – to the door), you should let him out at once and give him heaps of praise. However, many dogs do not catch on very quickly, much to their owners' frustration; in such cases, you will need to continue to think for your dog – taking him outside regularly and without fail.

Eventually, your adult dog will be able to reliably let you know when he wants to go outside, and will only need to defecate once or twice a day in the garden before being taken for his walks, and to urinate three or four times. If you notice any significant increase in your adult dog's need to urinate, seek veterinary advice, as a number of conditions can be responsible.

Your puppy will learn to ask to go outside.

Do not become complacent too early; you will still need to do the 'thinking' for your puppy.

ONE STEP BACK

Many people fall into the trap of getting complacent. They put in all the hard work during the first few months, taking the dog outside without fail at frequent set times throughout the day. Then, because the dog is always clean in the house – and perhaps has been for months on end – they start to stop being so vigilant, believing the pup is fully house-trained. This is where the problems can start.

It is understandable to think that a six- or seven-month-old would have cracked the rules after months of success. But, until your dog is nine to twelve months old, he will only be house-trained for as long as you continue to think for him – so don't cut corners too soon.

WHEN ACCIDENTS HAPPEN

Even if you are incredibly vigilant, and stick rigidly to the house-training schedule, you are bound to encounter the odd accident. It is important to clear away any evidence of the mishap at once, as your puppy will be tempted to return to the same spot if there is any trace of urine or faeces.

However, simply cleaning the area with disinfectant is not enough to discourage the pup. Although it may smell clean to a human nose, a canine nose (which is infinitely more sensitive) will be able to detect any trace of a scent. Ammonia-based cleaners can actually encourage a dog to repeat his misdemeanour, as, to a puppy nose, they smell very similar to urine.

To remove the accident thoroughly, use a proprietary cleaner (available from pet stores or vet surgeries), or use a little biological washing powder in warm water on the area, rinsing thoroughly afterwards. Check it on a hidden piece of carpet first, just in case it stains.

OUT WITH THE OLD

Whatever you do, never punish the dog for having an accident. Old-fashioned methods of 'rubbing the dog's nose in it' are incredibly cruel and will ruin your relationship with your dog. Plus, they don't work.

Even a milder form of punishment – like shouting at your dog – is counter-productive. All you will achieve is a dog that fears you, and is scared of going to the toilet in front of you. Consequently, the dog is more likely to eliminate in hidden places in the house, rather than outside in the garden or on walks. This is because he will associate his toileting with your wrath and so will do his very best not to relieve himself in your presence.

NOT GUILTY

Reprimanding the puppy when you discover one of his accidents is never effective, as the puppy will not associate your displeasure with something he did two hours ago, half an hour ago, or even two minutes ago. The puppy will not be able to connect the two events, and will instead associate your anger with whatever action he is doing when you make your discovery – whether he is playing in the garden, asleep, or whatever.

HOUSE-TRAINING

WHEN ACCIDENTS HAPPEN

"Aah," some people say, "but my puppy knows exactly what he has done wrong – you can see the guilt on his face!". This is a common misconception. The so-called look of guilt is actually one of fear, where the pup is trying to look as passive as possible. In the pup's eyes, his pack-leader is angry and he doesn't have the faintest idea why. However, the puppy knows that he has to show he isn't a threat, in order to appease his irate owner and to ensure he isn't harmed. So he looks as

Always reward positive behaviour so your puppy understands what is required.

submissive and appeasing as he can – and, sadly, this is often misinterpreted as guilt. Worse still, the pup may urinate to signal his submission (see opposite), and so anger his owner further.

POSITIVE BEHAVIOUR

Punishing negative behaviour is cruel and ineffective. Rewarding positive behaviour is kinder and is proven to work. If your pup *wants* to relieve himself outside, because he has associated it with being given a treat, or having a game afterwards, then you will be working with a willing pupil, rather than battling against a reluctant one. (See page 7.)

SUBMISSIVE URINATION

In canine language, submissive urination is a pup's way of saying "I am not a threat – I am urinating through fear and deference to you." Puppies are prone to submissive urination. Their size makes them vulnerable to everything around them, so they may disarm any perceived threats by immediately urinating when encountering an adult dog, a new human visitor etc. A submissive pup may also urinate when his owners return home.

Submissive urination is an entirely different subject area to house-training, and the pup's urination should not be treated as a toilet-training accident.

• Build up the pup's confidence. Never punish him; instead, reward good behaviour.

• Don't make a huge fuss of the pup when you return home, wait until he has calmed down.

• When you do finally pet him, kneel down to his level rather than stooping over him (which the pup may view as a dominant position).

• Always ignore the urination; do not respond at all. If necessary, greet the pup outside – you may be more relaxed about the urination if you know your carpets are not being ruined!

• Many pups grow out of submissive urination as they become more confident, but if the behaviour persists, seek the advice of a professional pet behaviourist.

Work at building up your puppy's confidence.

SCENT-MARKING

With some dogs, particularly entire adolescent males, urination is a statement of power. This relates to the male dog's scent-marking instincts to delineate his territory and to signal to others his ownership of it. You may notice that entire males will cock their legs numerous times throughout a walk. They aren't urinating because they need to, they are performing a kind of 'canine graffiti' – making a "Fido was 'ere" statement, and scribbling over an earlier "Rover was 'ere" in the process.

If you catch your dog scent-marking in the house, distract him by giving him some obedience exercises to do, rewarding any good responses. The cause of his behaviour will then need to be addressed.

CHANEL
ESSENCE
OF
HOUND

EQUAL RIGHTS

A small number of females scent-mark. As with male dogs, insecurity, or dominance (territoriality), can be root causes. A bitch may also scent-mark when she comes into season.

TACKLING THE CAUSE

If a new dog comes into your house, the resident dog may well feel threatened, and will assert his dominance by scent-marking. If this happens, reinforce your dog's dominant position over the new arrival (by letting him eat first, go through doors first etc.)

Neutering provides a solution where the scent-marking has a hormonal cause. It prevents dogs feeling so 'macho', and they no longer consider it necessary to defend their territory so vigorously against other dogs.

RESCUED DOGS

Rescued dogs (plus some show dogs and working dogs) that have been kennelled for any length of time can often experience a blip in their house-training. Confined to a pen, with limited access to a toileting area beyond their den, many dogs, through necessity, have to soil the area where they live, eat and sleep. After months of this, even years, they can sometimes find it difficult to adapt to a home environment where they must relearn the rules and refrain from eliminating indoors. The problem is not insurmountable, however. It is simply a matter of being patient.

Exactly the same principles are used when training an adult rescued dog, as are used when training a puppy. Devise a programme where the dog is taken out frequently throughout the day, and reward good behaviour. It is especially important that you use reward-based training, as the relationship with your rescued dog will be fragile to begin with, and you must not jeopardise the dog's trust by losing your temper.

NEVER TRAINED

Do not expect miracles. In some instances, the rescued dog may never have been house-trained in the first place. But you *can* teach an old dog new tricks. All they need is to be taught what is expected of them, and to receive the time and commitment needed to follow through a daily toileting schedule (page 5).

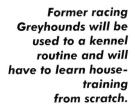

Former racing Greyhounds will be used to a kennel routine and will have to learn house-training from scratch.

ANXIOUS WETTERS

Moving to a new home is an anxious time for any dog, particularly one that may have become 'institutionalised' from long-term kennel confinement. The stress of a change of routine, a new environment, new faces, and new smells can all take their toll on a dog's continence.

In some cases, the dog may be urinating to make his new home his own. Surrounding himself with his own scent may be a rescue dog's 'comfort blanket', where, in the midst of so much newness, he has something familiar to settle himself.

HOPE

Usually, a rescue dog stops having accidents once he settles in and starts to feel he belongs in his new home. Given lots of love, most dogs no longer need to surround themselves in their own scent, and start to view their new home as their den, which should not be soiled (page 4).

If the accidents keep flowing, make sure the dog is checked over by a vet as there could be an underlying cause for the persistent incontinence (e.g. cystitis).

PROBLEM SOLVING

FAIR WEATHER FRIEND

BACKGROUND

Josie, a Whippet, joined her owner, Ruth Reynolds, when she was eight weeks old. Ruth had never owned a dog before, so she took the breeder's advice and worked hard at house-training. She used a crate at night, and lined it with comfortable bedding, and, in no time, Josie got the idea of being clean. She was naturally fastidious and did not want to soil her bed. The early work paid off, and by four months of age, Josie was house-trained.

PROBLEM

Unexpectedly, at the age of eight months, Josie started to urinate on the kitchen floor. There seemed to be no reason for this behaviour. Ruth had not changed her routine of taking Josie out to the garden – although she no longer stayed with her. She had not needed to do that since Josie was a very young puppy.

CAUSE

It took a bit of detective work, but, with the help of a dog trainer, Ruth found the cause of the problem. It was Josie's dislike of cold weather! When Ruth first took Josie from the breeder, it was late-spring and the weather was quite warm. Six months later, though, the late-autumn weather made the prospect of going out to the garden altogether unenticing. Because Ruth had left Josie on her own in the garden, she 'forgot' about toilet-training, and rushed back inside, to use the warm kitchen instead.

TREATMENT

Whippets are short-coated dogs that are particularly prone to the cold – and they usually hate the rain! The problem was tackled in two days.

Firstly, and most importantly, Ruth bought Josie a warm, waterproof coat. Josie took an immediate liking to this, and was only too happy to wear it. Secondly, Ruth took Josie out to the garden – and stayed with her. Correct behaviour was instantly rewarded, and Ruth had a game with Josie so that she was not intent on rushing straight back into the house.

In just a few days, the problem was solved. Josie was happy to go outside again, and she returned to being 100 per cent reliable in her house-training.

PROBLEM SOLVING

BABY BLUES

BACKGROUND

Bob, a five-year-old Golden Retriever, was the much-loved pet of Anna and George Harris, who had owned Bob since he was a pup. He was doted on, and never put a paw wrong.

PROBLEM

Bob started being dirty in the house just when his owners had their hands full with another problem – dealing with their newborn baby. Bob was checked over by a vet, but there was no physical cause for his incontinence.

CAUSE

Bob's problem was simple: his owners had become lax in their dog duties, and Bob was a little jealous of the attention the new arrival received. Rather than being a Golden Retriever, he was a very Green Retriever. Bob loved the new baby, but his big, wet nose was a little put out.

With the upheaval of having a demanding new baby in the house, the timing of Bob's walks became increasingly irregular. One night, when Anna and George were particularly late for a walk, Bob peed on the hall floor. Within moments, Anna and George were on the scene, apologising to poor Bob and taking him for an immediate walk to say sorry.

The next morning, Bob's walk was behind schedule once more, and he peed again, though this time probably as a deliberate act to attract his owners' attention and to get the walk he was so desperate for.

This behaviour continued, until, eventually, Bob was urinating four or five times a day – whenever he fancied his owners' undivided attention.

TREATMENT

Anna and George had to be retrained. Whenever Bob peed, they had to ignore him. At all other times, they should be attentive to Bob and to involve him more in their everyday life.

'Bob-time', when he had his owners exclusively to himself, was allocated throughout the day around the baby's schedule and feeding times. During 'Bob-times' Anna and George took it in turns to take Bob for a walk, play his favourite games, and tickle his tummy – Bob's favourite activities in life.

Within 10 days, Bob learned that peeing resulted in being ignored (the very opposite of what he hoped to achieve). He also realised that he didn't need to urinate to get attention – he was reliably given attention throughout the day. Bob wasn't the only one to benefit from the revised daily schedule. Anna and George also learned to love their 'time-out' from the baby, and the therapeutic time they could enjoy with baby number two – Bob.

OVER TO YOU...

If you stick to a frequent schedule, there should be no
reason why you can't have a fully house-trained pup in a
couple of weeks, or even in a matter of days. If you work
hard now, it will save you weeks of worry in the long-term,
and a fortune in replacement carpets.

Good luck!